Instant Poetry Frames
All About Me

by Betsy Franco

NEW YORK • TORONTO • LONDON • AUCKLAND • SYDNEY
MEXICO CITY • NEW DELHI • HONG KONG • BUENOS AIRES

Teaching *Resources*

For Alejandra

Cover design by Jason Robinson
Interior design by Sydney Wright
Interior illustrations by Maxie Chamblis, James Graham Hale, and Sydney Wright

ISBN-13: 978-0-439-57628-4
ISBN-10: 0-439-57628-8

2 3 4 5 6 7 8 9 10   40   15 14 13 12 11 10 09 08

Contents

Introduction

In *Instant Poetry Frames: All About Me*, primary poets are encouraged to flex their creativity muscles and stretch their poetry skills. All this is done in the context of fun-filled, engaging poetry frames and starters that ensure success for everyone.

The poetry frames in this book focus on the child's world—in and out of school—so they fit right into your social studies curriculum with no effort on your part. They are perfect for introducing, teaching, and reinforcing concepts and themes that your students are already studying.

The interesting and unique formats of the frames help children explore their world at home, school, and in the community—from family and friends to favorite book characters and foods. The frames help students describe the ups and downs of being who they are, create a table of contents of their life, predict what they might be like in the future, and more.

Additionally, the poetry frames vary in complexity and in the amount of student participation, allowing you to individualize instruction. Children are asked to add only a word or short phrase in some frames, while they write the entire poem in others.

What Are Poetry Frames?

Poetry frames are quick and easy reproducible "invitations" into the world of poetry. They are simple, unfinished poems that invite students to complete them. Some have missing words or phrases, others consist of blank lines with helpful questions and tips. All of the frames included in this collection give children the comfort of writing within a structure. They also provide visual clues to help young poets brainstorm ideas and illustrate their own poetry.

Why Use Poetry Frames?

To build writing skills and meet the language arts standards.

Confidence makes all the difference when a child is writing poetry. The structure of poetry frames gives students the support they need while developing a wide range of writing skills. Frames motivate young poets not only to write, but to keep writing! Using them helps children to:

* write in a variety of poetry forms
* organize their ideas
* sequence events
* use pictures to describe text
* focus on specific parts of speech
* apply mechanical conventions to their writing

* write for a variety of purposes (to entertain, inform, explain, and describe)
* edit and "publish" their work
* use prewriting strategies to plan written work
* and much more!

To present a variety of poetic forms.

In this collection, you'll find formal and informal poetic forms including a blues poem, a letter poem, and an acrostic poem. There are also engaging frames for writing a list poem, a two-word poem, an ode, visual (or concrete) poems, and poems that give directions.

To individualize instruction.

The different frames require varying degrees of participation from students. Some ask children to fill in words, and others invite them to write an entire poem. This variation allows you to individualize instruction because it enables everyone to participate at his or her own level.

To encourage self-expression.

Using poetry frames enables students to share their opinions, feelings, and imaginations about themselves, family, friends, and the world around them. Children are, for example, encouraged to describe themselves, write about their favorite season, explore their feelings, examine their routines, imagine themselves as animals, and express what family and friends mean to them. In addition, students are invited to let their imaginations run loose and get downright silly when they describe a goofy day, tell what they would do if they could be any book character, and imagine the wild things they would do if they were one of the seasons of the year. The frames also guide children in writing about their preferences, memories, and life experiences. As they develop and personalize the poems, students can explore their lives and cultures, share details about their experiences, and express their imaginations.

To introduce basic elements of poetry.

Elements or poetic language are purposely interwoven throughout this book. Examples of personification, alliteration, metaphor, simile, and neologisms (made-up words) are included. Students are invited to use fun action words and interesting describing words to paint pictures with their language. They are also encouraged to play with different parts of speech—naming words (nouns), describing words (adjectives), and action words (verbs).

To build awareness of rhyme, rhythm, and repetition.

Poetry frames are simply poems that need to be finished. They are structured so that they will be fun to write and read aloud when completed. They often have a pattern of repeated phrase, or rhyming couplets or quatrains to begin and end poems. Some poems rhyme throughout, but in most cases, children don't have to worry about the rhyming—they can just enjoy reading their poems after completing them.

To integrate language arts, math, and science into your social studies curriculum.

Poetry can so easily embrace the rest of the curriculum. In this collection, students learn important social studies concepts as they explore their feelings, favorites, and preferences about many areas of their lives. They write about friends and family, describe their perfect bedroom, tell about places they like to go, and even give directions on how to find them. Math skills are reinforced in the frame "If There Were Two of Me!" Children learn about science subjects with poems such as "If I Were an Animal," "My Favorite Season," and "If My Shadow Didn't Copy Me."

Using the Frames in Your Classroom

Each poem can be written individually, with partners, or as a class collaboration. Here's how you might use the frames with children:

1. Copy the frame of your choice for each student. Introduce the frame with the group before children begin. Review the directions together and write an example as a class.
2. Provide students with a copy of the reproducible frame and have them use pencils and crayons or markers to fill it in.
3. Circulate around the room to check that each child is engaged, helping to brainstorm when needed.

After poems are completed, celebrate kids' efforts by inviting them to:

* share their poem with a partner or a small group
* read their poem to the class or to an older buddy
* copy their poem onto a blank sheet of paper and illustrate it as part of a display
* make their poems into a class collaborative book for the classroom library
* display their poems on bulletin boards
* take home and share their poems with families
* write their poems on blank strips, display them in a pocket chart, and chant them with the class
* act out their poems
* create their very own anthologies by binding all their poems together
* hold a poetry reading in which each child reads his or her poem to the whole class

Connections to the Language Arts Standards

The activities in this book are designed to support you in meeting the following standards outlined by Mid-continent Research for Education and Learning (McREL), an organization that collects and synthesizes national and state standards.

Uses the general skills and strategies of the writing process:

* Uses writing and other methods (e.g., using letters or phonetically spelled words, telling, dictating, making lists) to describe familiar persons, places, objects, or experiences
* Writes in a variety of forms or genres
* Writes for different purposes (to entertain, inform, learn, communicate ideas)

Uses the stylistic and rhetorical aspects of writing:

* Uses descriptive words to convey, clarify, and enhance ideas
* Uses a variety of sentence structures in writing

Uses grammatical and mechanical conventions in written compositions:

* Uses conventions of print in writing (upper- and lowercase letters, spaces between words, writes from left-to-right and top-to-bottom)
* Uses complete sentences
* Uses nouns, verbs, adjectives, and adverbs in writing

* Uses conventions of spelling in writing (spells high frequency, commonly misspelled words from appropriate grade-level list; spells phonetically regular words; uses letter-sound relationships; spells basic short vowel, long vowel, r-controlled, and consonant blend patterns)
* Uses conventions of capitalization and punctuation in writing

Uses the general skills and strategies of the reading process:

* Uses mental images based on pictures and print to aid in comprehension of text
* Uses basic elements of phonetic analysis (common letter/sound relationships, beginning and ending consonants, vowel sounds, blends, word patterns) to decode unknown words
* Uses basic elements of structural analysis (syllables, compound words, spelling patterns) to decode unknown words
* Understands level-appropriate sight words and vocabulary
* Uses self-correction strategies (searches for cues, identifies miscues, rereads, asks for help)
* Reads aloud familiar stories, poems, and passages with fluency and expression
* Understands the ways in which language is used in literary texts (personification, alliteration, onomatopoeia, simile, metaphor, imagery, rhythm)

Source: Kendall, J. S., & Marzano, R. J. (2004). *Content knowledge: A compendium of standards and benchmarks for K–12 education.* Aurora, CO: Mid-continent Research for Education and Learning. Online database: http://www.mcrel.org/standards-benchmarks

Instant Poetry Frames

All About Me

Write a poem to describe yourself.
Fill in the blanks with words that tell about you.
Draw a picture of yourself in the mirror.

In the Mirror

When I look in the mirror,
here's what I see:

Two _____ eyes looking at me,

a great big smile,

and _____, _____ hair.

And _____

and _____

are what I wear.

My _____

is something special about me.

I really like the *me* I see!

by _____

In this poem, describe yourself.
Use only two words in each line.
Draw a picture of yourself.
Examples: *swims laps*
sleeps late
twirls hair
reads comics

Two-Word Poem About Me

If I
used only
two words
on each
line to
describe me,
here's what
those words
would be:

_____ .

_____ .

_____ .

_____ .

_____

That's me!

by _____

What are some things you think about?
Write a visual poem about what goes on in your mind.
Use the questions in the box to help you get started.

What do you . . .
* think about in school?
* think about eating?
* hope to do after school?
* wish for?
* worry about?
* daydream about?

Reading My Mind

There are thoughts in my mind almost all the time.

I think about

I think about

I think about

I think about

I think about

These are some things I think about!

by _____

A poem is more interesting if the poet is honest about himself or herself.
Tell about yourself. Write your poem on the lines. Save your best idea for last.

The Ups and Downs of Being Me

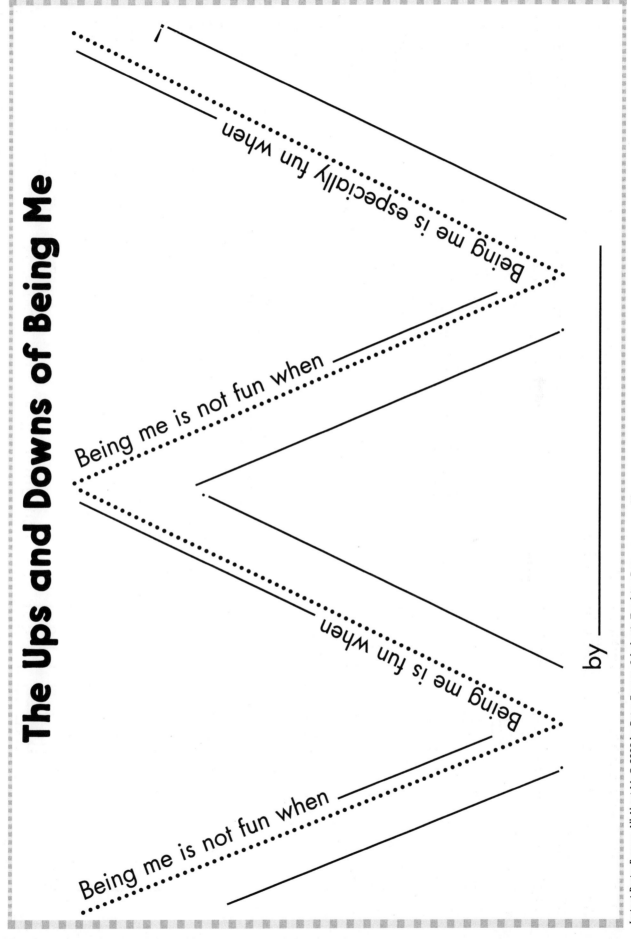

Being me is especially fun when

Being me is not fun when

Being me is fun when

Being me is not fun when

by

Instant Poetry Frames: All About Me © 2008 by Betsy Franco, Scholastic Teaching Resources, page 11

Imagine you have a special box.
Describe the favorite things you would you put in it.
Save the most special or surprising thing for last.

Examples: *my stuffed giraffe with the ripped ear*
a heart-shaped rock from the beach

My Special Box

Some people might collect a small glass dog,
a computer game, a big ball of string.
In my special box, what would I have?
Well, I'd collect all sorts of things:

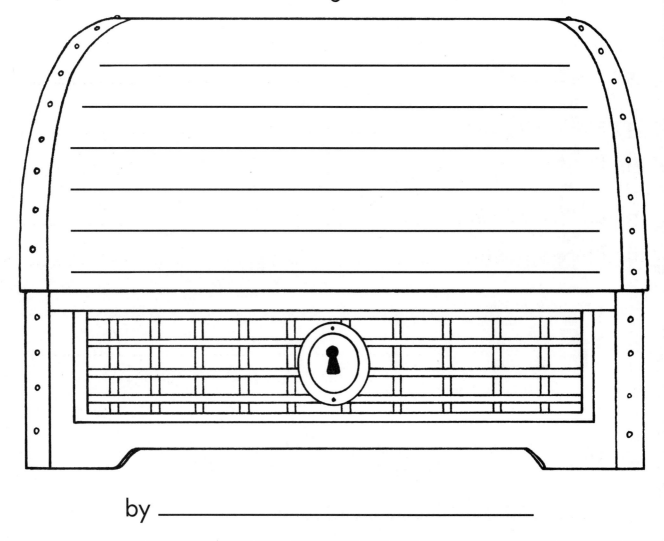

by _____

Everyone has many feelings. Many of those feelings are opposites.
Write about the opposite sides of you!
Then draw yourself showing two opposite feelings.

Different Sides of Me

I'm scared when _____,

but I'm brave when _____.

I'm sad when _____,

but I'm happy when _____.

I'm excited when _____,

but I'm calm when _____.

I'm serious when _____,

but I'm silly when _____.

My feelings are deep.
My feelings are wide.
I've got many feelings side by side.

by _____

Pretend you are your favorite season. What kinds of things would you do?
You can do *anything* you want—real or wild.
Draw pictures to go with your poem.

Examples: *If I were the fall, I'd paint the green leaves gold, red, and orange.*
If I were the winter, I'd close school and let everyone go sledding.
If I were the spring, I'd have purple flowers falling from the sky.

My Favorite Season

If I were the _____,

I'd _____.

I'd _____.

I'd _____.

I'd _____.

I'd _____.

That's what I'd do

if I were the _____.

by _____

   Instant Poetry Frames: All About Me © 2008 by Betsy Franco, Scholastic Teaching Resources

What are your favorite foods?

Use alliteration—write words that begin with the same sound.

Save your favorite for last.

Then draw your favorite foods around the poem.

Example: _chewy, chocolate chip cookies_

Favorite Foods

_____,

I could eat that food _every_ day!

_____,

I never leave a crumb to throw away.

_____,

What a wonderful, scrumptious treat.

_____,

That's my favorite food to eat!

by _____

Think about when you get ready for school.
What sounds do you hear?
Make up words for the sounds to use in your poem.
Draw pictures to go with your poem.
Example: **bling bling** *for the school bell*

School Morning Sounds

_____, _____,

I hear my alarm.

_____, _____,

I eat my breakfast.

_____, _____,

I brush my teeth.

_____, _____,

I put on my clothes.

_____, _____,

I zip my backpack.

_____, _____,

I travel to school.

_____, _____,

I walk into the school.

Bling, bling,
the first bell rings!

by _____

In this poem, you can exaggerate!
Be wild and silly and fun.

Example: *I would be your friend*
even if you had spaghetti for hair.
I would be your friend
even if you liked to eat mustard and jelly bean sandwiches.

I Will Always Be Your Friend

I would be your friend
even if _____
_____.

I would be your friend
even if _____
_____.

I would be your friend
even if _____
_____.

I would be your friend
even if _____
_____.

I would be your friend
even if _____
_____.

Yep! I will always be your friend!

by _____

Think about the clothes you wear at different times.
Write a poem about them!
Draw pictures, too.

What I Wear

If you ask me what I wear,
it really depends on where.

I wear _____

when _____ .

I wear _____

when _____ .

But I just couldn't do without my favorite

_____ !

I wish I could wear it everywhere!

by _____

   Instant Poetry Frames: All About Me © 2008 by Betsy Franco, Scholastic Teaching Resources

If you could be any book character, who would you be?

What would you do?

Use your imagination to write about your experiences.

Draw your character on the book.

My Favorite Book Character

If I could hop into a book and be a character—ANYONE—

I'd choose _____, that's who I'd pick,

because being _____ would be lots of fun.

I'd _____.

I'd _____.

I'd get to _____,
which I've never done.

I'd _____.

I'd _____.

There's no comparison, _____ is definitely the one!

by _____

Pick a memory to write on the first line of the poem.
Describe your memory on the other lines.

Try to remember:

* what happened   * who was there
* how you felt   * sounds, sights, and smells

Example:

I remember the first time I jumped off the high board at the pool.
I remember bubbles exploding around me as I plunged into the water.

I Remember

I remember _____

_____.

I remember _____

_____.

I remember _____

_____.

I remember _____

_____.

Inside of me,
stored away,
memories can seem
as real as today.

by _____

Write a poem that is a quiz about your favorite things.
Fill in the blanks.
Make sure one of the answers is correct for each line.

Quiz About Me

Is _____ or _____
my favorite book?

Is _____ or _____
what I like to eat or cook?

Is _____ or _____
my favorite kind of pet?

Is _____ or _____
the most exciting person I ever met?

Is _____ or _____
my favorite color of all?

Which is my favorite season: _____,

_____, _____, or fall?

by _____

Instant Poetry Frames: All About Me © 2008 by Betsy Franco, Scholastic Teaching Resources

Fill in the blank with the name of your favorite wheels to ride.

Write about your wheels on the loopy lines.

Things to consider about your wheels:

* how fast they go   * how they sound
* how they look   * where they go

My Wheels

The wheels on my _____

are very big deals. They

My wheels spin with me on top until we get to a place to STOP!

by _____

Your shadow is a copycat. It does everything you do.
But what if it had a mind of its own? What would it do?
First, think of lively things you might do.
Then tell what your shadow would do differently.

If My Shadow Didn't Copy Me

When I would pick apples from the tree,
    my shadow would catch them on the ground.

When I would run a race,
    my shadow would cheer me on.

When I would _____

    my shadow would _____.

When I would _____

    my shadow would _____.

When I would _____

    my shadow would _____.

It would be fun if once in a while
    my shadow did something new.

But I like it a lot that my shadow does
    whatever I like to do!

by _____

Make an acrostic crossword poem about your family.
Think about:

* what your family does together
* words that describe your family
* where your family goes together
* how you feel about your family

M

Y

F

A

M

I

L

Y

by _____

Instant Poetry Frames: All About Me © 2008 by Betsy Franco, Scholastic Teaching Resources

Imagine everything in nature celebrated your birthday.
What would each part of nature do?
Do not use more than three words on a line.
Draw pictures to go with your poem.

Example: *The lightning would*
write my name
in a neon
flashing streak.

If Nature Celebrated My Birthday

The _____ would

_____

_____

_____.

The _____ would

_____

_____

_____.

The _____ would

_____

_____

_____.

All for my birthday!

by _____

Use your imagination to make up an ice cream treat.
It can be yummy or yucky!
In the first and last blanks write the word "best" or "worst."
Draw a picture of your treat, too!

Recipe for My Ice Cream Treat

If you follow these directions, your results will be first-rate.

You'll say, "This is the very _____ treat that I ever ate!"

First, add _____.

Next, mix in _____,

a dab of _____,

a handful of _____,

and a gob of _____.

Now you're done preparing
and you're ready to dig in and eat

the very, very _____ ever
ice cream treat!

by _____

Instant Poetry Frames: All About Me © 2008 by Betsy Franco, Scholastic Teaching Resources

Imagine what you could do if there were two of you.
Write a poem that is silly or serious—or both!
Then draw yourself—twice!

If There Were Two of Me!

If there were two of me
then I could fit
a lot in one day—
Just think of it!

I could _____

and _____
at the very same time.

I could _____

and _____.
Now that would be fine.

I could _____

while I _____
when I was at school.

I could _____

while I _____.
How incredibly cool!

It's fun to think about two of me.
Just imagine if there were three!

by _____

In a blues poem, you're allowed to complain.
Write three complaints. Repeat each one.
Example: *I feel blue when*
I keep missing the soccer net.
I feel blue when
I keep missing the soccer net.

The Blues

I feel blue when

_____.

I feel blue when

_____.

I feel blue when

I have to _____.

I feel blue when

I have to _____.

I feel blue when

I can't _____.

I feel blue when

I can't _____.

Tomorrow will be a better day.
Tomorrow will be a better day!

by _____

Instant Poetry Frames: All About Me © 2008 by Betsy Franco, Scholastic Teaching Resources

Write a poem to compare yourself to things in nature.

Make each sentence interesting.

Example: *I am April rain plinking on the roof.*
I am the wind whispering through the trees.

Ideas

* forest * thunder
* ocean   * star
* sunshine * comet

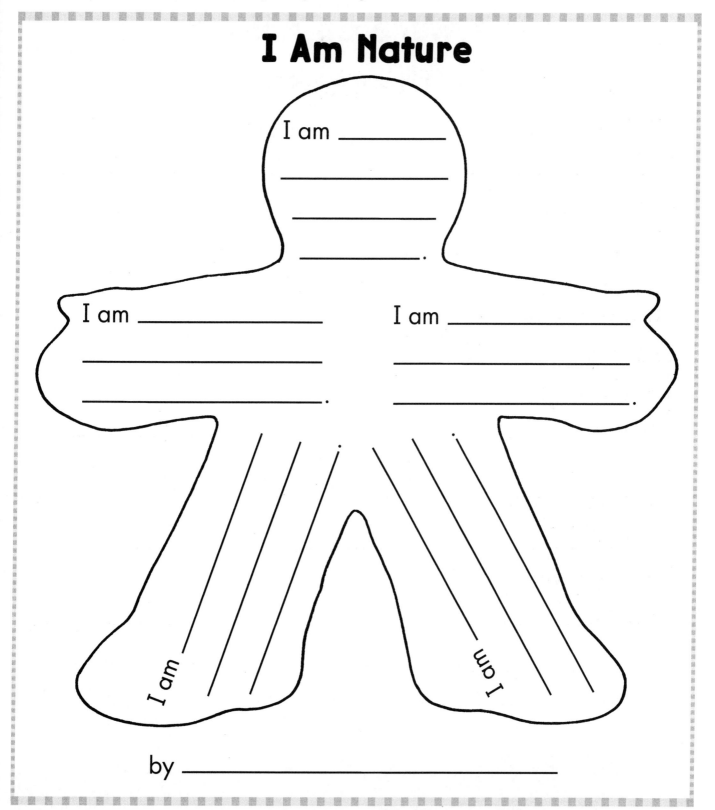

I Am Nature

I am _____

_____

_____

_____.

I am _____

_____

_____.

I am _____

_____

_____.

I am _____

I am _____

by _____

Imagine that you could be an animal.
What kind would you be?
Describe what you would do.
Draw yourself as that animal.

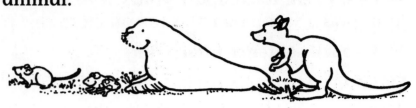

If I Were an Animal

If I could have scales, feathers, skin or fur,

I'd be a _____.
That's for sure.

I'd sleep _____.

I'd eat _____.

I'd say, "_____."

When I move, I'd _____.

I'd be good at _____.
That's for sure.

If I were any kind of animal in nature,

I'd be a _____.
That's for sure!

by _____

Imagine you are one of your favorite pieces of clothing.

Your poem will be a letter to you from this piece of clothing.

Write your name in the first blank.

Write your clothing's name on the second line and at the end of the letter.

Think about what your clothing would:

* complain about   * want you to do differently

* be happy about   * want you to know about its life

A Letter From My Clothes

Dear _____,

I am your _____.

I _____

_____.

I _____

_____.

I _____

_____.

I _____

_____.

And one last thing:

I _____

_____.

Sincerely,

_____

by _____

Suppose you wrote a book about your life.
What would you put in the Table of Contents?
Fill in the blanks with things that happened to you at different times in your life.
Example: *Chapter 3: When I Was a Little Kid*
Learned to Ride a Bike
Broke My Arm

Table of Contents of My Life

Chapter 1: When I Was a Baby

_____

_____

Chapter 2: My Family

_____

_____

Chapter 3: When I Was a Little Kid

_____

_____

Chapter 4: When I Was in School

_____

_____

To be continued . . .

by _____

   Instant Poetry Frames: All About Me © 2008 by Betsy Franco, Scholastic Teaching Resources

In a rap poem, the poet brags about himself or herself.
Write a poem to brag about yourself. Exaggerate!
Draw a picture to go with your poem.

Example:

I am so handsome, all the birds whistle as I walk by.

ME!

I am so _____

_____.

I am so _____

_____.

I am so _____

_____.

I am so _____

_____.

I am so _____

_____.

I am so _____,

the moon shines its light only on me when I finally go to bed!

by _____

Imagine you could decorate a room.
What would it look like? What would be in it?
Write your poem in the shape of a room.

Example:

My room has a petting zoo in one

down one wall.

corner and a

It has a water bed and
swimming pool in the middle.

TV in the other. A waterfall cascades

* Ideas *

* movie theater
* library
* amusement park
* playground
* snowy hill

A Tour of My Perfect Room

by _____

Where would you like to go to be alone or relax?
Write the name of your special place in the title.
Use words that paint a picture to describe your place.
Then draw your special place.

Example: *My special place is as quiet as*
a hang glider sailing in the wind.

My Special Place: _____

My special place is as _____ as _____

_____.

It makes me feel _____.

I hear _____.

I smell _____
when I am there.

I taste _____.

I touch _____.
That's why this is my special place.

by _____

What are some of your favorite things to have and do?
Look for pictures of these things in magazines.
Cut them out and glue them onto this page.
Leave room under, around, or in the middle
of the pictures to write a poem about yourself.

Patchwork Poem

by _____

Write a poem about someone in your family.
Write that person's name in the title.
Picture in your mind what the person
is often doing.
Use details to describe what you see.
Then draw a picture of that person.

My _____

_____

_____

_____.

Or _____

_____

_____.

Or _____

_____

_____.

by _____

Read the plain poem in the box.
Then rewrite the poem.
Use words that paint lively pictures.

Things to think about:
* what the kids remind you of
* *exactly* what they are doing
* other words to use for "rings" and "run"

Example:
Kids are buzzing around like
a beehive without a queen bee.

Before School Starts

_____

_____

_____

_____

_____

_____

by _____

Instant Poetry Frames: All About Me © 2008 by Betsy Franco, Scholastic Teaching Resources

Imagine you get really goofy one day a year.
Write about the things you would do!

On Goofy Day

I'd put shoes on my hands
and gloves on my feet.
I'd brush my teeth
while I eat.
I'd _____

_____

_____

_____.

I'd _____

_____

_____

_____.

I'd _____

_____

_____

_____.

I'd be nutty and goofy
in so many ways.
That's why they would call it
Goofy Day.

by _____

Think about things you like to do and where you do them.
Write directions that tell where someone might find you.
Also tell about what you might be doing at each place.

Example: *Turn right at the soccer net and you might find me kicking a goal.*
Go straight for a mile and turn left at the ice cream parlor where
I might be ordering a chocolate chip ice cream with sprinkles.

Directions for Finding Me

Are you looking for me?
Here's where I might be:

_____

_____

_____

_____

_____

_____

_____

Follow those directions
and look around.
There are places to find me
all over town.

by _____

Instant Poetry Frames: All About Me © 2008 by Betsy Franco, Scholastic Teaching Resources

Sometimes a poem is shaped to look like what it tells about.
This poem is about a loose tooth.

My tooth is loose
  My tooth is
    My tooth
      My

    tooth!

Write a poem that looks like what it tells about.

Picture Poem

by _____

Write a poem about what you like to do on:

* a summer day   * a winter day
* a rainy day   * a birthday
* a Saturday   * a windy day

Write the kind of day in the title.
Use action words to write your poem.
Then draw a picture about your poem.

Example:

What I Like to Do on a Summer Day
Build sand castles
Throw a baseball
Sit in the sun
Eat barbecue
Drink lemonade
Ride waves
All day long!

What I Like to Do on a

_____

_____

_____

_____

_____

_____

All day long!

by _____

A prickly emotion is a feeling that makes you mad, sad, or scared.

Write a prickly emotion in the first blank of the poem.

Use these questions to help you write about your prickly emotion:

* How does it feel?
* When do you feel this way?
* Does it get you in trouble? How?
* How is it uncomfortable?
* What do you do when you feel this way?
* Does it ever help you?

Prickly Emotions
* anger
* embarrassment
* disappointment
* sadness
* fear
* jealousy

Example:

My anger is as fierce as a cornered cobra snake.
I feel angry when my big sister teases me.
Sometimes I scream and shout.

My Prickly Emotion

My _____ is as _____ as

_____.

_____

_____

_____

_____

_____

_____

by _____

Instant Poetry Frames: All About Me © 2008 by Betsy Franco, Scholastic Teaching Resources

An ode is a poem that praises a person, place, or thing.

Example: *My friend is summer—bright and full of energy.*
My friend is a swift, graceful antelope.

Use these questions to help you write an ode that describes a friend:

✳ What season is your friend? Why?

✳ What kind of animal or growing thing is your friend? Why?

✳ What kind of food is your friend? Why?

✳ What color does your friend remind you of? Why?

Draw a picture of your friend, too.

Ode to My Friend

My friend _____

_____.

My friend _____

_____.

My friend _____

_____.

My friend _____

_____.

Although my ode is about to end,
my friend will always be my friend.

by _____

Instant Poetry Frames: All About Me © 2008 by Betsy Franco, Scholastic Teaching Resources

Write a short story about a pet that you have or wish you had.
Write the kind of pet in the title.
Describe what it is like—its looks, personality, and funny or cute things it does.
Then underline about 12 words in the story.
Use the words to write a poem.

My Pet _____

_____

_____

_____

_____

_____

_____

My Pet _____ **Poem**

_____

_____

_____

_____

_____

_____

by _____

What do you wish you could change about yourself?
What do you like most about yourself?
Fill in each line to finish the poem.
Draw a picture of yourself.

All About Me

I wish I were better at _____,

but I'm glad I'm so _____.

I wish I _____,

but I'm proud I'm so _____.

I wish I were _____,

but I'm lucky I'm so _____.

There are always things
I'd like to change or trade,
but I'm very happy
with the way I'm made!

by _____

If you could see yourself all grown up in the future, what would you see?
Complete each line.
Draw a picture of yourself in the future.

Things to think about:
* What you do for fun
* If you are famous
* What you are really good at
* What adventures you have
* What kind of work you do
* If you have a family

If I Could See Into the Future

If I could see into the future,
what would I see?

I'm _____.

I'm _____.

I'm _____.

I'm _____.

I'm _____.

If I could look into the future
that's how my life might be.
I guess someday when I'm grown up,
that's when I'll really see.

by _____

Notes